boy

for my sister Margaret and brother Garry

*To Maurice
with love,
admiration and
appreciation from
the*

boy

enns

victor enns

May 8, 2012

HAGIOS PRESS
Box 33024 Cathedral PO
Regina SK S4T 7X2
www.hagiospress.com

Copyright © 2012 Victor Enns

All rights reserved. No part of this publication may be reproduced, stored in a retrieval system, or transmitted in any form or by any means without the prior written permission of the publisher or by licensed agreement with Access: The Canadian Copyright Licensing Agency. Exceptions will be made in the case of a reviewer, who may quote brief passages in a review to print in a magazine or newspaper, broadcast on radio or television, or post on the Internet.

Library and Archives Canada Cataloguing in Publication

Enns, Victor, 1955–
   Boy / Victor Enns.

Poems.
ISBN 978-1-926710-14-3

    I. Title.

PS8559.N57B69 2012   C811'.54   C2012-901524-5

Edited by Paul Wilson.
Designed and typeset by Donald Ward.
Cover art: "Ducks or Rabbits," woodcut print by Allen Hessler.
Cover design by Tania Wolk, Go Giraffe Go Inc.
Set in Minion Pro.
Printed and Bound in Canada.

The publishers gratefully acknowledge the assistance of the Saskatchewan Arts Board and The Canada Council for the Arts in the production of this book.

ACKNOWLEDGEMENTS

Thanks to Lynn, Alden, Theo, Bronwyn, Jo, Darcy, Peter, Gerhard, and Ted Dyck, John Weier, CVII, Prairie Fire, and the Manitoba Arts Council.

CONTENTS

Guilty   9
Burn down the house   10
Highway 14a   11
Where's my horse?   13
Well water   14
Learning to read   15
The cistern   17
The furnace room   18
Kitchen   19
The dining room   20
Living room   21
Father's study   22
This wheel's on fire   23
My brother's bedroom   24
My brother gets his license   25
My sister's bedroom   26
Escape artist   27
In the hayloft   28
Graduation   28
Summer school   30
Shit house   31
Red rover   32
Milking   33
P. J. Schaefer's funeral   34
Sawatzky takes a picture   35
Preparation   36
Doctor Boreskie gives me a needle in the ass   37
So new a house   38
Gimme shelter   39

Recess   40
The golden hour   41
Jesus Christ my personal saviour   42
Too many stupid Mennonite boys   43
Desire   44
Desire 2   45
Border crossing   46
Change room   47
Transistor radio   48
Cap guns   49
The sugar-beet war   50
Planets   51
Raft   52
Getting my hair cut   53
Twiddler hands me deliverance   54
Salvation   55
There is dust in the air   56
Windbreak   57
My sister's Jewish boyfriend   58
Rabbit bones   59
Raspberries   60
My sister's Anglican boyfriend   61
Astronaut in training   62
Blackboard love   63
My sister's Catholic boyfriend   64
I dry the dishes   65
Delivering pancakes   66
Brace   68
Football in the afternoon   69
Falling in love with Barbara Loeppkey   70
The last shall be first   71

Giving them the slip   72
Dancer   73
Kites   74
Inner resources   75
Taking my bicycle   76
House arrest   77
My afternoon with Teddy Green and Ted Harris   78
Johnny Cash   79
The dig   82
Bibliophiles   83
Chuvalo raises his fists   84
Eric Bueckert knows his cars   85
Older women   86
Mrs. Pieper asks me in   87
Wiener roast   88
Shooting sparrow hawks   89
Weeding beets   90
Beggar   91
I only want to be with you   92
So how much does it matter?   93
No thank you   97
The shoes of the fisherman   98
Here we are   99
Leaving   100
Experienced   101
Under the leaves   103

GUILTY

I know
I am
on the day

I learn
to say
mum.

I think,
know,
I am

bad. My teeth
mark
her breast.

Look
at her
eyes.

BURN DOWN THE HOUSE

I run.

Black and white
speed boots raise dust
from the acre garden,
me with nowhere to go
but back in the house.

Mother better
be there. I see
her now. She tugs
the Electrolux.

I slam
the outdoors
behind me,

reach hungrily
to mum
in that floral
print dress

again. She moves to me
this time, catches fire.
I see
her now

nothing but fire
between us,
ashes

I remain.

HIGHWAY 14A

I am left behind.
Bereft, I don't realize
until she's gone.

My feet, sandaled,
smaller
than a disciple's,

push on the pedals
of the red & white trike.
I am on my way.

No one is at school.
My dad in the garden,
mum on her way

to Altona, and the laundromat
before running water.
I race after her.

Pounding the pedals
under the sun on highway 14A,
making my way

after her, to
grab her soul
pull her

back to me
one more time.
A farmer

figures I'm
too young for the road
pulls me over.

Returns me
to my father
in his garden.

WHERE'S MY HORSE?

Mother vanishes
out the back
door, seen too late,
out of the corner
of my eye.
She gets away, clean

this time. I'm just
a four-year old
cowboy. I ride
my spring horse palomino.
I ride it
into the ground.

WELL WATER

1.

The pump sends its arms down
to nether nether land.

It raises the cold sweet taste of minerals
from a hole deeper than my father's soul.

This is what I need my fifth summer, the cool water
from cowboy songs, the metal dipper in my hand.

I wet my lips, douse my head
refresh my body, ward off the dead.

2.

My sister grabs my hands,
my brother, my feet.

I am younger, by years
and the only one getting wet.

They dip me into the plastic pool
I begged my parents for —

some water in the summer time,
some cool, clear water,

with the notion of god
sky blue in my eyes.

LEARNING TO READ

1.

In the beginning
all there is
is blur.

Mum refuses to believe
I am stupid.
She pulls my ear

to be sure.
The optometrist
swings

the black mask
in front of my face —
the lenses click away

stigmatism, give me
a new one
to wear.

2.

Black horn rimmed glasses
arrive in a small brown box
my name on the label,

let me see —

the letters making words
make sense to me.
I am five,

in short pants —
pulling up my socks, next to mum
who loves me, on the front stoop.

She looks over
my shoulder,
a book in my hands.

THE CISTERN

I can't believe, so easily,
it is under my feet.

There is no river to be brought.
There is no river to be bought.

The heavy man brings water,
his tank full from the town spout.

The cistern is in the basement,
to the right of the stairs.

There's a pump in the kitchen,
to fill the metal bowl.

There's never enough
water to wash sin away

John the Baptist's head
on a plate.

THE FURNACE ROOM

To the left of the stairs
the green fire-breathing
furnace, eating coal.

Insatiable, the flames
call to me.
I throw in bitumen.

The shroud of dust
rises from the coal bin,
cloaks my invisibility.

No-one knows I'm down here.
I like to play with fire.
Sometimes I get away.

KITCHEN

This is the origin of good
smells. The oven is wired

and so am I. Wait
for the white *verinka*,[1] on the boil.

The Jersey cream gravy bubbles,
thickens, fresh, with butter.

The farmer sausage sweats
mother's roasting pan.

The two quart Mason jar
of dill pickles on the arborite table.

Sitting on my hands I wait
to put it all together.

Fork to my mouth
after the amen of grace —

heaven
on my tongue.

---

1   Mennonite for cottage cheese perogies

THE DINING ROOM

Only for Sunday
or birthdays
unless I'm riding
my spring horse
in the corner.

There are patterns
in the linoleum
under my back,
I push off —
slide, to the other side

of this birthday.
No one remembers
to pick up
Cokes at the Co-op;
Sun-up a poor
substitute.

Wishes leave
me breathless,
my friends
leave me
embarrassed.

Too old for the spring
horse, too young
to reign
in my pony.

LIVING ROOM

My mother and my sister
do their living here.

Behind the white door
my mum studies and writes her essays

in plain English, too blunt
for a really good grade

with me pounding
on the door, crying

Mama ich will rein!
Mama ich will rein![2]

Later, waiting for sleep
I hear my sister play Chopin.

---

2   Mama, I want to come in!

FATHER'S STUDY

His is the room with his Bibles,
the strap in the roll-top desk.

He meditates and writes sermons,
the open door to the verandah

lets in the summer air. The sun sets
over the town. God's in his

heaven as I look
for mine.

THIS WHEEL'S ON FIRE

Goethe and Schiller are on fire
it's too late for the volunteer brigade
the library's going up in smoke.

I see the tongues of flame
half a mile away
in the middle of the night.

I throw shadows
in my parent's bedroom —
breathe

the words, *the school
is burning down
can you see the light*?

MY BROTHER'S BEDROOM

My brother sits on his knobby bedspread
with a Brylcreemed wave in his hair,

studies a book in his hand. I want
his age; meantime

old toys will do,
Meccano stored

under the bed, and me too clumsy
to make anything work

when he leaves it to me.
No amount of waiting will

fix the weight of Jesus
tightening the bolts.

MY BROTHER GETS HIS LICENSE

The vehicle licensing bureau is a desk
in the front room of a house on Berlin Street.

My brother is sixteen, and already
wearing jeans though James Dean is dead.

My brother drives mother's Studebaker,
not some fancy-assed Porsche.

"Do you know how to drive?"
"Yes"

"How did you learn?"
"My Dad taught me."

"Did you? Frank, does he know how?"
"I did. He does."

*"That'll be sixteen dollars, now stay out of trouble
don't make me sorry I gave you this."*

A thump of the rubber stamp and it's done.
He can drive. He is legal. He is free,

only the sweater girl
to restrain him.

MY SISTER'S BEDROOM

She will not play with the dolls
my mother bought. Mum

only had homemade, and my sister
doesn't care that these

are store bought, including the
Bride's Doll that can walk

if you hold her hand. My sister
is unhappy and leaves

the dolls on her bed, takes
her books and her charms

to the world in Winnipeg
where she learns.

She leaves
her room empty

me all of six
when she goes.

ESCAPE ARTIST

I caught Him
when he wasn't
looking, but he
got away, my hands
empty for prayer. Some
self-deliverance
touches me,
there, there
and
there.

IN THE HAYLOFT

It must be important,
you have to show me. Or —
I want to stay and watch.
You lie on your stomach across
the hay bales, a wide strategic gap
for your hands on your penis.
All my life, I carry this image —
see you jerk your cock, your face twisting,
your breath caught short. You leave
your leavings in the hay.
It must be important,
you have to show me.
I am too young to know.

GRADUATION

She knows the answers are not here,
ready to leave.

There is no dancing;

just circle games, hasty refrains
of B–I–N–G–O, black

pants and white crinolines,
satisfying no-one. Put out

she knows more than
she'll tell, expelled with

the book under her arm
the snake underfoot.

SUMMER SCHOOL

Dad peels, boils, slices white potatoes
sliver thin, slides them into the hot buttered pan.

He is alone and looking after this boy
who hates to get his hands dirty.

The first half of the day is father's
usually given to the garden

weeds, or raspberries, the heat raising
a sweat on father and son.

The afternoon is given to the boy
who orders books, and loves to read.

Mother is at summer school, learning
to get to where she wants;

sister and brother
out of this new house while

dad shifts the potatoes with a spatula
lifting the golden brown, butter dripping potatoes.

Cracking brown eggs on the edge of the pan
he stirs them into our dinner.

There is no-one else in the room; the sun still hot
at six o'clock. The cat on the window sill, purring.

SHIT HOUSE

Two weeks my sister is in charge,
my brother, not responsible.

My friend and I come out of the outhouse
we two, giggling with beans freshly stuck

up each others bums, playing in the stink
of the summer, transgression

still new in our hands.
Sister recoils, slaps

my jeering face
me already forgetting

what I have done.

RED ROVER

I lock myself in
the blue Studebaker.

I look out the window,
I see the red rubber ball

tear up
the lucid sky,

clear the roof of the barn
where my mother was born.

I curl up in the back seat
a firm grip on *Little Lord Fauntleroy*.

The children chant,
run circles.

I sit very still, imagine
words for rescue.

MILKING

I follow my dad
to the barn first thing.

Only one brown cow this summer
waits for milking.

Dad has the wooden stool
under him, cow teats firmly in hand.

Hear the milk squirt into the steel
pail, the occasional miss

directed at the cat, or at me leaning
against the wall.

The pail of warm milk
is strained through a cheesecloth.

I hurry the milk to the house,
scoop a cup for my

cereal. This is what is left
of his farming, his love

in the morning.

P. J. SCHAEFER'S FUNERAL

This dead
body is forever
gone. I didn't know him
but learn now my parents
will leave
more than once,
one day forever,
me here
under this cottonwood
weeping.

SAWATZKY TAKES A PICTURE

The couch like Freud's, we are
arranged as though baptism
could happen soon.

I wear a white shirt
I wear a white bow tie
I wear white shorts,

my Oedipus in bloom.

PREPARATION

The old house is gone.
what's left, a hole in the ground.

I stand next to my father.
I stand next to the foundation.

The old house is gone,
my boy hands dry in the dust.

I strike the mortar with a hammer,
free the brick placed in 1892.

The old house is gone,
My red wagon collects the debris.

I load out the sand coloured bricks,
I take 24 up the grade, pile them in the sun.

The old house is gone,
I slip two bits

allowance
into my pocket.

DOCTOR BORESKIE GIVES ME A NEEDLE IN THE ASS

Mum takes me to the doctor's office,
there, right next to the barber's

with shades on the window
so no-one can see

me bend over, the smell
of antiseptic in the air.

He seems like a gentleman,
offers reassurances —

(damn the nurse swabbing my buttock)

jabs my ass with a needle
for something mum feared —

(damn Doctor Boreski giving me a needle in the ass).

As I pull up my pants, all three
look the other way.

SO NEW A HOUSE

English was easier than what I learned
at home until television changed all that.

It was so new a house. The bungalow
I watched grow out of the ground.

Mother's coffee and cookies
store-bought, on the lips of the working men.

This house with two indoor washrooms, upstairs
and down, running water for hand-washing and bathing.

I can be left alone downstairs in the rec room
with books and television, hours and hours

everyone is busy, there is a separate
peace in it. My quiet acceptance of a place

nobody else wants
to own.

GIMME SHELTER

First, huddle under the school desks
in five rows of six.

I look at the girls to see if any of them
are afraid, to see if any of them will

show their underpants
to the end of the world.

The siren signals
apocalypse.

Two hundred children
run through the streets of Gretna,

try to find their nuclear families,
to put arms around us all.

Let us find shelter,
home at last.

The Americans bombed Hiroshima
The Americans bombed Nagaski.

The missile silos just
miles away.

RECESS

The public school,
a long concrete bungalow —

from nowhere to
nowhere.

We're let out for 15 minutes —
time cut so fine.

The bristling sun takes
no breaks, hot on our backs.

There will be tests
here on the outside.

I keep distance
from boys calling names,

talk about a catholic God
with McKillican,

his asthma as much of a bully joke
as my Jello belly.

Taunts nag like crows
on the telephone line.

We circle the schoolyard —
wait for the bell.

THE GOLDEN HOUR

The sun isn't going to kill me as
I walk down the boundary road in 1963,

kick stones, dust rises, the light shifts
around my busy feet.

Heat slips between my legs,
my thighs, neighbours, after all.

The Americans on the other side
are dangerous. Military observers

deliver war overseas, discontented soldiers
kill. At home, Presidents die, televised.

I can't know this, and what little I know
I keep to myself. There are not many places to hide;

the sun shines, romances the western horizon,
lights blond hairs on my skinny boy legs.

I walk on, the slip of grass between my thumbs.
My breath calls water birds to this dry land.

JESUS CHRIST MY PERSONAL SAVIOUR

Sin + the devil
one summer night.

The wooden plank
under her light

summer dress.
Me on the other

side, looking
for Jesus

and sanctuary
in the converted

airplane hangar.
I say yes

to the Brunk brothers'
invitation to holy flight.

My parents never went.
Saved already

+ their prayers
heaven sent.

TOO MANY STUPID MENNONITE BOYS

want to touch my sister's
tits, their erring hands

coming up empty. They
don't understand.

She wants more than
they can offer

the dust of the town
in the cuffs of their pants.

She looks for sophistication
but does not dance.

Moving to the city
her heart set on romance.

Here are men, not boys,
who can buy her dinner;

play trumpet
in bars.

DESIRE

A hot Sunday
afternoon and we play
behind the abandoned
barn where the pigs are bled.

I am the doctor telling you
to drop your pants
lie on the examining table
this spot of grass will do.

I am to give you
an injection,
that is what doctors
do. Your white bum

waits for the prick
of the needle, my thumb
pressed through the second and third
finger, before my hand opens

like a disease across your
soft buttocks. I fall
from my knees, beside you
make love to the earth

for all I am
worth, is lost
in that
discovery.

DESIRE 2

I am in love
with the Schellenberg twins.
They're from the farm
and wear dresses to school.

Green jumpers, above the knee
socks pulled up white
against their white calves,
feet in white canvass sneakers.

I can't choose, and try to learn
by guessing. I'm wrong
half the time. So
throwing caution to the winds

I buy two packs of Wrigley's Doublemint
and before their bus arrives from Silberfeld
place them on their desks. One for Judy
and one for Joyce. My career

as a secret admirer underway.
I begin to understand
gift, romance — but mostly
the stirring in my pants.

BORDER CROSSING

Me and Grant Klassen are on our bikes.
We meet at the Shell station across from the water tower.

We move on, traveling around
the curve with towels round our necks.

We pass our white clapboard customs house just built.
We wave to Penny Batchelor's dad working there.

We cross the line to the United States
of America and Babe Ruth chocolate bars.

We identify ourselves to strangers.
We don't know any Americans,

even if we see them every day,
here at the crossings

in their brick customs office
with, rumour has it, guns inside.

We are Canucks, and the Yankees let us in;
the sun as hot on their side where we go to swim.

CHANGE ROOM

God I never invoke
but could, looking for

safe passage
through the Neche change room.

Strip, face the concrete block
walls open to the blue sky —

a wooden bench running
around the room. Hairier teenage boys

look at my little boy
dick and asshole —

can't wiggle my trunks
on fast enough.

American boys, just before
Vietnam, leave slight

bruises on my ass with
the echo of the snapping towel.

I smell the chlorine,
make a run for it —

hear the lifeguard shout
feel the air make room

for me moving water
with my cannonball —

sunlight glitters in the spray
through the chain link fence.

TRANSISTOR RADIO

Small enough, could be red, could be
wrapped in brown leather
with a short silver antenna feeling
for the Beatles and Herman's Hermits
in summer sun.

Dust on the road fouls
mother's clean linen on the line.
Walking home from the neighbours
I hum a song without a clue
the devil's on my shoulder.

Short pants and bubble gum
chips and Coke from Pete's,
the street that grows me
has lots of broadleaf shade
to keep me from burning.

CAP GUNS

Who could be so lucky
as to have a pair
of cap guns, holstered

round his hips. A real Indian
from Roseau River in the trees.
We play on three and a half acres.

I don't give him
a gun. I have two pistols
and a white Winchester carbine.

His bow
and arrow
no match

for a well-armed
preacher's kid forgetting
Christ one Sunday afternoon.

THE SUGAR-BEET WAR

There are two piles of sugar beets
next to the track, waiting for the train.

The one-armed loader silhouetted
to the west, until we get close,

hear the sound
of huge drying fans

in the air. Loren and I climb a pile,
his dad inspecting for rot and disease

while we clear trenches and take
aim, lob beet mortars arcing in the sun.

I take a direct hit, my face as surprised
as my brain that drops me where I stand.

The loss of consciousness
proves I am a man.

PLANETS

Dark is where I begin
to smell the roots of my disaster.
Garden dirt still
in my shoes. No runaway love,
to clasp me to her bosom, just
these booted teenage boys, one
swift kick in the balls
helps me remember
my place
in the universe.

RAFT

Build my own ark,
sink my own self.

Rubber boots fill with cold
water, railroad ties

heavy with tar
my dreams left

for nothing
on the side

of the ditch
with dirty snow.

GETTING MY HAIR CUT

Sid Lesperance cuts hair in Gretna,
a two-chair shop, but just the one barber.

The story goes
he learned to cut hair in the Army.

The way he cuts
boys' hair makes it so.

No one is sure, but there are whispers
he may be French, or even worse.

I don't care, I read
comic books, openly.

This the only place I may,
sit in a red chair waiting my turn,

skip the Bible stories, and Prince Valiant,
look for something funny, a free laugh.

In the chair I am raised up, smell
Sid, blue Barbicide dripping from the comb.

TWIDDLER HANDS ME DELIVERANCE

I am as familiar with Box 184
as anyone in my family.

The Post Office smells of the government
brick walls and stone floors

wickets with bars as if there
still were bandits in these parts

to surprise Twiddler playing with his
thumbs. I slide him my green parcel card.

He hands me a padded
envelope stuffed with books

to take me away
take me away from here,

this weather station
I call home.

SALVATION

I knew early on, my Messiah
was the word, the word made
flesh, alphabet
coming to my rescue
once I had glasses
and could tell
the letters apart. Salvation came
in a brown envelope
from the University of Manitoba
extension library. I read
my way out of a place
as small as the eye
of a needle and as full
of itself as a bag of dirt.

THERE IS DUST IN THE AIR

and it's not even July,
dust scrolls behind the Coronet
follows me to church.

Hallelujah brother!
Jesus wants me
in the Dodge dealer's car.

There's four of us
in the back seat.
I catch a glimpse

of skin under Julie's skirt,
she's under dressed
for the hereafter.

I know her underpants
don't cover enough
as she sticks to the vinyl.

Here we come, scattering
gravel, dust in the ditch
on the Russian thistle.

Sunday school up ahead,
nothing but dust
devils left behind.

WINDBREAK

We dig a hole
line it with cardboard
cover it with prairie
brush, scrabbled from
the windbreak.

We hide
from the grown-ups
who pretend
they have no idea
we smoke

deadwood cigarettes,
look at glossy pictures
of naked women
in the dirt.

MY SISTER'S JEWISH BOYFRIEND

The impresario brings my sister home one Saturday
morning in his black T-Bird convertible.

She's just a young thing, snug in the red leather
interior, her country family outside, making hay.

He casts himself in the farmer's daughter porno
hoping to get in my sister's pants. Instead

the pitchman finds himself in the hayloft,
my brother taking his T-Bird for a spin —

brother has just got his license and his own
girls he loves to take for a ride.

The heavyweight stands at the loft door, waiting,
for a something to hang on to, and put in its place.

My father's at the bottom of the conveyor,
sending up the bales.

My sister is in the house,
making lunch and talking to Mum

about this Lothario
trying to get under her skirts.

This Saturday morning in July,
is haloed by the sun in the red barn.

And I, watching in the filtered hay
light, take flight.

RABBIT BONES

The morning
after I left
the top of the cage
open
the baby rabbits
were gone.

Little bones
in the barn
scattered, the cats
now hiding
in the long grass.

RASPBERRIES

Birds do little harm
to raspberries buried in their bushes,

prefer strawberries splayed
against the hot grey earth.

We set out dishes of water
to distract them. They are after all,

thirsty. Juice of red berries, plucked from the
vine, sweet as the sin of television.

The raspberries, now they are mine.
Every other day I claim the fruit.

Stick my bare arms into the rows
of green and thorn, my head, shaved and bowed

my red fingers,
in and out,

pray the season is over soon,
so I can retreat to the cool of the fall.

In the meantime, red raspberries in my bowl
awash in Jersey cream, a waltz on the radio.

MY SISTER'S ANGLICAN BOYFRIEND

This other summer, my sister is engaged
to a rich Anglican boy

with a cottage on Lake of the Woods.
He speaks as if what he says

matters, when everyone is watching
to see what he will do. He does his

best in a sweater vest, getting warm in
his long sleeves, keeping his complaints

to himself. Compared to biblical tests
picking raspberries isn't much, but it's more than he can bear.

My sister feels his pain, picks the thorns from his fingers
returns the ring. She sends him back

to his Daddy, where he does the best he can with
gin & tonic, and a round at the Club.

I finish his row.

ASTRONAUT IN TRAINING

This town, a long
way from Cape Kennedy.

In short pants he walks
home with me, Apollo

on the launch pad, cameras
mounted, ready to broadcast

live. He knows his astronauts,
at six has begun training

for his assured trip
to Mars.

Ten years later. His Dad's Meteor
parked on a grassy knoll.

Monoxide carries him weightless
through to the other sky.

BLACKBOARD LOVE

Now
is it her
or her sister
with the bad kidney
that I knee
in the back
her smirk toward
the blackboard
my name
and another
in a chalk heart
I want
erased.
I got
the strap, hers
a shorter
sentence.

MY SISTER'S CATHOLIC BOY FRIEND

They met at the conservatory of music
each giving lessons, with what they learned before.

He played what he could hear
she played what she could read.

He was from around the mountain
she was from the prairie plain.

He played trumpet in Winnipeg clubs,
she played piano for the choir.

He had the authority to order food and wine
when they went to Rae & Jerry's.

She had the authority to say no
or yes when it was time.

They did not practice religion,
love a purer sign.

I DRY THE DISHES

Side by side
with mum
I dry the dishes.

It gets dark, the window
faces east to the pasture
and the garden.

We've eaten dinner
and the house seems empty
father, mother, and son.

My brother and sister
have left, we hardly
rate as a village;

five hundred souls wait
for the Second Coming,
eyes on their bank books.

Mum sees the time
as time for my bath.
We have running water.

I take off my clothes
and slouch
in hot water.

After, mum offers
me a towel,
my penis erect.

DELIVERING PANCAKES

I deliver pancakes hot out of the pan
to Miss Wall who lives alone in a small white house

up our street
and might need something to eat.

She is terribly thin
and has forgotten who I am.

When she answers the door
not much to see, all the blinds are drawn.

She draws me in to the shaded living
room, takes the crepes from my hands

collapses at my feet. I am afraid
to touch her. I run faster than on field day.

I scream to my mother that Miss Wall
is dead. Mum takes the pan from the element

and hurries away. I'm alone in the kitchen
waiting to hear about the death of Miss Wall.

I eye the stack of crepes ready for lunch
wonder how long until I eat,

with Miss Wall dead and all, maybe
I could have one pancake while they take her away.

My mum comes back says she found Miss Wall
on her knees wolfing down pancakes as if the world

would come to an end. Her time in the house,
surrounded by flowers, ends with a flurry

of dollar bills falling out of newspapers, wallpaper,
mattresses, old socks in the hall, the smell

of African violets
in the air.

BRACE

Polio is more than a scare
in our neighborhood.
The shoemaker's son has a brace,
and his hair is long.

No idea, where this comes from,
no idea, where this goes, the vaccine
too late. The son knows, *I've got
a leg shorter than the other.*

The night before the game
He oils his glove, wraps the sealer
ring hard around the leather. Dreams
of catching a fly ball

without the glint of silver
in the sun. The end of the day
in his eye, the game
so nearly won.

FOOTBALL IN THE AFTERNOON

I'm not allowed to play.
Even outside

the league, my teacher parents protect
me. I like books enough, but I want

a Kenny Ploen spiral
in my hands, me

taking the ball
to the end zone,

Winnipeg Stadium crowd
on their feet with a roar.

What I've got
is Harry dogging me.

I slip past the lilacs,
Rob gets the ball to me.

A rare touchdown in Gerhard's yard,
for me, a receiver in short pants

crossing the line. The sun is warm
and I'm standing in glory

this one time.

FALLING IN LOVE WITH BARBARA LOEPPKEY

Blue eyes, and blonde hair in a wave like my sister,
fine blonde hair on her arms

in the sleeveless cotton top with buttons
up the front every boy in town

imagines under his fingers. She does her best
not to notice like my sister,

but in school a bit of a disappointment,
she works so very hard.

I can never figure out a way
to help with her English and Social Studies,

Math's too much for me to grasp,
but I want to hold her slim young body,

crush her 13 year-old breasts
against my shirt while I smell her hair.

THE LAST SHALL BE FIRST

Beyond recess, this is phys ed
and the teacher announces me
and the other fat boy, who
is the last chosen;

we will be choosing.
It's the end of the world
as the jocks know it
who will dip our heads

into flush toilets, a new torture,
still pacing town, when
the teachers
have their backs turned.

But this day, This day I say —
You over there. I'll play third.
I take line drives
and sliding monsters

in stride, I hold
my ground. My body
understands supremacy,
my mind says —

Who are you kidding?
But this week, one
out of 52 my body
is in charge.

Boy

GIVING THEM THE SLIP

The boys make me
the goat, and take me
for a lamb.

Here I am,
I say,
here I am.

Turn the other cheek
as fast as I can
get down the street.

Around the corner
this lucky afternoon
I slip away.

I run down
the Pastor, who
understands

the name of this game.
Salvation, I say
you should know.

The devils are on
my heels,
I better go.

DANCER

I see your black
tail swish goodbye —

me suspended breathless
from a tree bough,

the air absorbing
your neigh. Hoof beats

fade in my heart,
in my ears.

It's all I can do
to hold on.

KITES

Butcher's paper, willow and string
I can never fly.

On the other side of the fence
The neighbour boys have sheets

of heavy plastic and all the nylon tail
I wish for.

Kites big as dreams
I can hardly see

their translucent skin
twist against my harboured sins.

Look up now, four o'clock
sun on my squinting face.

the rustle of robes + ten
commandments in my ears.

INNER RESOURCES

I learn to remove
the window.

My parent's have learned
to lock the doors.

They have given me
the key, often forgotten.

I set the screen aside,
straddle the sill

pull myself
inside.

I know how
to make

Campbell's tomato soup
from the can.

The milk is cow fresh
from this morning.

Christie crackers crumble
in my fist.

I am safe, here,
inside the house,

a spoon
in my hand.

TAKING MY BICYCLE

I sell you a pumpkin
and deliver it, orange,
in the basket of my bicycle.

Amazing what a quarter
gets you
in 1965.

The dirt road there
and back, sunset's
just a minute away.

Too late,
my mum and dad
keep buying me watches.

Watch me lean my bike
up against it,
the house new as tv.

HOUSE ARREST

I am late and beaten
for it. Then hand in hand

shown the exact boundaries
I must honour.

My father and my mother
cannot be afraid —

I might be in the wrong place
at the wrong time,

what would they do
with my injuries?

Better I was safe
at home.

MY AFTERNOON WITH TEDDY GREEN AND TED HARRIS

I'm allowed
to go to the Queens Hotel.

The owners are French, rumored to have
a connection to the Canadiens.

I desert the Maple Leafs, to enjoy
the Canadiens dynasty. My apostasy

earns me the disregard
of every boy in town,

but this summer Saturday
this day, we have Ted Green and Ted Harris

cooling their heels in the bar
of the Queens hotel with their Molson's

and I am there. The autographs
as unlikely as the owner's son

masturbating his dog
under the table.

JOHNNY CASH

True to form
I leave
the car when
I get hungry.

We are somewhere
in Peace River country.
Only my parents know
how to get to that farmyard.

I wear my
red & blue Carnaby St.
wool pants with white stars
running up my legs.

My t-shirt is red mesh and sleeveless
full of little round
holes, my nipples
jauntily say hello Alberta!

The boy in overalls
has gotta be
younger than me, and look
his head is shaved. Ha. Ha.

What does he know? His parents
are gone for two days.
They've left him in charge of
all that they have to keep them
for the winter.

He serves us buns and coffee,
the butter he churned
this morning. He is ahead
of me.

In the living
room he swings
the record needle
over the spinning vinyl

It's not the Beatles,
hell no
It's Johnny Cash,
I don't know

nothing
I don't know shit
I've been listening to a.m.
twisting the dial.

There's none of that up here,
Johnny walks out
of Folsom, with the country
blues again. I can barely hear
this story

My cousin sits back
and says *let's thank
God for shotguns
and Johnny Cash.*

*Yesterday I shot this bear
coming toward the calf
on a rope, unknowingly
I had set bait.*

*I blew out the bear's heart
Once or twice, he was
as surprised as I was.
I have what's left
hanging from a rope.*

*It was Johnny who was here
for me, who had a song to sing
when I had blessed blue nothing
but a dead bear to string.*

*Let us pray
Say Amen!*

THE DIG

I keep coming back to this:

I watch my father and brother
dig a new shit-hole
for the outhouse.
I am the first to see
the skull and bones.

Again and again: my father
and my brother uncover the world
in our backyard, for me to see
fine fine hair
scalp in a spade.

I gather these fragments
in an apple crate
mother & child
skull & bones.

Just my luck
them digging in
our own backyard
to uncover an unfathered family
lying dead under the green green trees.

BIBLIOPHILES

We are on the prowl, you and I
in the basement where my sister
keeps her private things when
she leaves town.

We find a box of books, now
understand, we are readers of some
renown, bright boys, we know
the secrets often found perfect bound.

We stumble across a cover, something
we've never seen: a woman,
bursts out of a bustier, a whip
slashes across her cheek.

The very idea this could be left behind,
could be in the house, right here
under mum and dad's bedroom
brings us to our knees.

She may have borrowed something from the Impressario's
impressive collection. It may be French,
something existential she's learned in school
but we know my sister's going to hell,

with us right behind.

CHUVALO RAISES HIS FISTS

My dad and me
watched the Canadian
champion. Television
still new in the house.
Fifteen rounds
a first for the newly named
Muhammed Ali;
George not paying
any attention
to anything but
staying on his feet
doing his impression
of a brick wall
graffiti on the way.

ERIC BUECKERT KNOWS HIS CARS

He can name anything
driving by, gravel road
or Highway 14A.

His dad's the car dealer
who opened the new town garage
with a flutter of flags.

There's little left
of Falk's old Esso station,
just old men and

the smell of oil
gas and grease
from the empty garage.

He lives just up the street
and his dad's as sharp
as a blade of grass. Business is good,

the fittest survive
as the town says
a slow goodbye.

Eric names the cars
that roll by our window
on our way out of town.

OLDER WOMEN

No friend's mother
makes me hard, no matter
what they wear or what they cook.

I look at girls my age,
fresh legs, and faces that
call in the rain.

I threaten them with love.
They misunderstand,
believe it's all a game.

My sister, the one exception,
ten years older and
the most beautiful girl

in town. Until tonight,
when
she catches the train.

MRS. PIEPER ASKS ME IN

She's in the yard
with a rake, when I walk by
throwing the hardball in my glove.

She asks me in for lemonade.
She wants me to play
the organ in her parlour.

All I want is to smell
the leather on my hand
and get away. But

I have been taught
to defer to my elders,
and be polite to the lonely.

I cannot play
but the simplest tune,
still she's happy.

She brings me lemonade
and pound cake. There's
nothing I can do

to make the clock
run faster or bring her
children and husband home.

WIENER ROAST

September and
school is back.

My parent teachers bring
other people's children

to our big backyard
with trees that touch forever

and never let
me down.

I am there
with the teenagers

black leather jackets
saddle shoes

none of us ever been
to a movie

but me grateful
to be here

in the smoke of
the poplar fire

this evening in a class
of my own.

SHOOTING SPARROW HAWKS

They perch on the very tops
of our 100 year-old cottonwoods

a long way up, with no idea
of the sadness on the ground.

Dad has the single shot.
Lets me try a few times,

but I never kill anything
he the better shot,

throws the feathered carcass
on the manure pile to rot.

WEEDING BEETS

This prairie ground grows sugar
rooted in dirt and promises.

No machines, people
to clean the rows.

Mexicans, poor Mennonites and me
saving for a saddle.

Sun fills the land
colours my back brown.

Kool-Aid in my thermos
at the end of the row.

I keep moving, hands
hardening on the hoe.

Three acres, three days and $90 later
I've had enough. Dad

takes me from the field
to the city and Birt Saddlery.

The muscular smell of leather
lets me know I'm in the world of men.

I have earned this place
but cannot hold.

BEGGAR

Take me to the river,
I beg.
Take me to the lake,
I beg,
Take me to the water,
I beg.

Summer on
summer my desire
searches for a beachhead
among the Bibles +
sugar beets,
vacation such an English word.

There are more lakes
in Manitoba than God
can count. I want to go
to any one of them
without chores or
lessons to learn.

This one summer
after years of campaigning
mum and dad take me
to the lake leaving
my brother at home to do
the chores for money.

At the lake
in my red t-shirt
and blue shorts my
hair burned blonde by sun.
I am where I want to be,
stupid as a ball of string.

I ONLY WANT TO BE WITH YOU

What does he see
in me?

He watches me
on the dock, his
eyes fishing.

I bait my hook,
the worm inviting
sunfish, perch.

Head of short blonde
hair, nowhere
else, but here.

He wants,
sing it Dusty,
he only wants

to be with me. He lies
to be with me.
His eyes

see my ass
under my shorts,
his eyes

snap his penis
erect, he fondles
his knife as he

takes a look,
love, really
not the issue.

SO HOW MUCH DOES IT MATTER?

1.

I ask.

Father gives me
permission
to go
fishing.

This unshaven
man has a license
to fish,
takes me.

2.

Jesus not on
this boat.

I remember
my Bible verses +

the fear of men
on the water.

So much I have
to learn.

3.

He solicits
my confession,
puts me

in a corner
with my pants
down.

4.

The stranger pushes me
into the bush ahead of him
self and his knife.

He is soon
naked. On this rock
of Canadian Shield

he wants me
to kiss him, stubble rough
on my other cheek.

I don't want to
know what he's
talking about.

Nothing I've learned
from my Father
prepares me;

I fall back to Bible
stories, I think
Ok God, I know

I'm guilty,

*but here is where
we could really use
a goat.*

5.

It's my fault +
my confession
brings me here,

but I cannot bring
myself to love
this man.

Unsatisfied,
he pulls me
up as he stands.

*"Turn around!
Show me
your little boy ass."*

6.

He stands behind
me in the spruce
scented air

fish knife in one
hand, his prick
in the other.

I turn, my short pants
in the moss, my y-fronts white
around my sneakers,

my eyes
on the far shore,
his kisses in my hair.

7.

Each stroke
a threat

on the long
way home.

I get there.
So does he.

8.

Back on the dock
I walk up the plank
without grace.

I cannot look
upon my father's
face.

NO THANK YOU

Father moves us
to the other
side of the road.

Now we are next
to the big lake
and I'm

out in it.

Soon I've gone
far past
the point.

I can hardly drag
this heavy
rowboat

back to the shore,
falls falling
to the right.

I refuse
rescue
I want no help.

On the water
the wind
in my face.

THE SHOES OF THE FISHERMAN

Father's shoes
crunch the shells

as he crosses
the stony beach,
me out of reach —

looking. But I work,
I know it's only
work

will bring me
to him. I
clear the point

near enough
now he steps
over the raucous water

clears the gunnels,
into the boat.
Father, saviour

takes on the oars,
my shame light
on his shoulders.

My life
in his hands.

HERE WE ARE

The worms are moving
and I'm going too.

I'm out early
in the morning sun.

A trowel in one hand
coffee can in the other.

The worms are
moving, and I am too.

I don't know
anything 'bout the city

but think it's the right
place for me. Subdivision

Red River gumbo
worm jamboree.

This is our lot +
my mother's new house.

Dad sees garden,
thinks apricots;

watches me pack
mud on my boots.

The **worms** are here,
I am, **too.** Subdivision

Red **River gumbo**
worm **jamboree**.

LEAVING

There is only one way
out of here, United States a mean prospect,

no, the only way to leave is highway 14A
to Highway 14 to Kern's corner

a hard left down Highway 75
a fast road cross the flood plain

on a good day with crops green
on either side leaving the past

a century behind.

EXPERIENCED

The blistering sun directly overhead, the summer of 1969.
My parents are gone for the weekend.

You, my skinny blonde friend, moved
to this worldly city a year before me

stand on the driveway, hand me
a tab of windowpane acid. I drop it

on the concrete and it's lost forever.
There is another and another

which we put on the tips of each
other's tongues and we melt away.

Inside we listen to Jimi Hendrix, Janis Joplin,
Jefferson Airplane on the Grundig cabinet hi-fi

as the world expands, and us
in it. Our faces meld with the copper

firewood carrier, flat on our backs
on the Persian rug in this Fort Richmond

suburb. When we can stand
again we go for a walk

alongside the Red River, trees
bowing before us, summer

as endless as our minds. Lost
I lose you and find my way home.

Alone, coming down, I phone you
and you whisper to me, tell me

to have a drink from my parents'
cupboard, a little brandy to take off

the edge in the dark. I never see
you again.

UNDER THE LEAVES

The Gretna yard is still
the place I dream from

where it's always summer
and the smell of grass

lies under the patterns of leaves
from one hundred year old trees

and me just here
reading in the landscape

ten years of sympathy
my back against it

feel the breath
the crosswind

of God for which
I was prepared

fiction
in my hands.

Victor Enns was born in Winnipeg in 1955. Raised in the small border town, often mentioned in weather reports, of Gretna, Manitoba, he moved back to the big city with his parents in 1968.

His hometown reclaimed him for his studies at the Mennonite Collegiate Institute where he graduated with its largest class in 1972; his mother's Studebaker stuck in low gear on the way to the party after graduation.

His first collection, *Jimmy Bang Poems* (Turnstone 1979), the result of his participation in an advanced creative writing workshop led by Robert Kroetsch, was published after his graduation from the University of Manitoba.

Boy is a prequel of sorts to *Correct in this Culture* (5th House, 1985) and *Lucky* Man (Hagios, 2005) which was nominated for the 2005 McNally Robinson Manitoba Book of the Year Award.